Super Brain. Super Life.

Train your Brain, and it will Change Your Life: Simple and Productive Exercises for the Brain and Memory

Benjamin Wood

Introduction

The brain contains millions of neurons (also called brain cells) that are necessary for our learning, cognition and memory retention. However, neurons die, and the brain does not generate more of it unlike other cells in the body. This can lead to memory loss and the reduction of our cognitive skills. From the moment that we are born, we lose few neurons, and the death of brain cells does not stop only until our death.

Although scary as it may sound, losing neurons is not such as bad thing, and it is a crucial part of the healthy function of the brain. The cells in our bodies undergo a programmed cell death which is also called apoptosis. It is important to take note that brain cells are quite metabolically expensive for the brain to maintain thus it needs to keep getting inputs as well as send signals in order to avoid being engulfed by the body through apoptosis. The thing is that it needs to be used. Otherwise, it will get culled. In fact, the neurons that you have left can actually take care of everything that you need to learn and remember for the rest of your life. The trick here is how to keep your brain healthy.

There are many ways to keep your brain healthy but aside from proper diet and getting enough sleep; brain training is a great way to maintain or improve your neural connections. The thing is that if you exercise your brain, it fires up signals to the neurons thus creating more branches called neural connections that can help you remember things, prevent cognitive loss and also improve your learning capabilities. Thus, this book will discuss what it is that you need to know about brain training.

Thank you for purchasing my book, it is my sincere hope it will answer your question on title.

Table of Contents

Chapter 1: The Basics of Brain Training

Since the beginning of time, our ancestors have been brain training themselves by doing their daily tasks. In fact, brain training has resulted to better cognition, and this is the reason why we are enjoying modern comforts. The thing is that brain training has allowed our ancestors to think of inventions and innovations that can make our lives better

Train Your Brain

Most individuals tend to forget that mental fitness is as necessary as physical fitness, and even require more care as compared to other body parts. Mental fitness is just as crucial, and it is often ignored. The brain training programs may be a great way to help to maintain overall mental health. Those who have already participated in several brain training sessions will be able to recognize the real benefits. These programs, which help in showing cognitive improvements, are intended to have long-term benefits.

Why train your brain?

Brain training involves all those exercises that are practiced by individuals to enable overall fitness of the brain. In real terms, everything that people do in their lives is in some way or other be considered as brain training. Although Brain training in the true sense is a set of scientifically designed activities or defined exercises that while being fun to practice also have several benefits if executed on a regular basis. The key elements of brain training sessions are to visualize on those improved performances through repetitive usage. By undergoing through various ranges of exercises which are set on different testing categories and designed on different mental capabilities and for various areas of the brain, the results of brain training programs can be really enjoyable.

Even though there are several hearsay and conjectures with regards to training your brain, there are quite detailed reports and research of the benefits of performing several activities that improve the functions of the brain. This will help in keeping the brain active and improving several specific metal functions which help in improving memory, concentration, and alertness. These brain training sessions will also help in improving the overall improvement of both left and right brain.

Lumosity and its benefits

The programs are effective procedures for elevating the quality of brain. These help in developing the memory capability and uplifting the confidence level. One of the efficient ways of maintaining the overall fitness of brain is through Lumosity. This new program has been developed by medical experts in neuroscience and cognitive psychology. The main aim of Lumosity is to stimulate the cognitive functions and organize in clinical patterns. This technique may be followed by all which helps in enhancing memory, concentration, and awareness. There is a huge line of scientifically developed games which may be categorized under different schemes such as speed, flexibility, memory, attention, and solving problems.

Staying mentally active is one of the most protective factors against age-related cognitive decline.

Keeping busy and staying social can contribute towards maintaining good brain health but what else should you be doing to protect your brain from age decline?

Research has proven that cognitive abilities can be improved and rebuilt by adopting and maintaining regular mental challenges. It is never too late to start, and it is fun to do.

In fact, a study conducted by neuro-psychologist Dr. Robert Wilson of the Rush University Medical Centre in 2010 claimed that brain exercise could defer the onset of Alzheimer's disease.

Also, studies proved elsewhere that brain training with elderly drivers resulted in an impressive 37% accident reduction in the over 70's.

It's interesting to note that games like crossword puzzles, number puzzles, and online brain training programs are unlikely to improve your higher-order thinking skills a great deal, although they are definitely worth incorporating into your brain training program.

For maximum brain health, you should be focusing more on problem-solving, decision making, planning, and higher-order reasoning. These activities challenge your mind on a greater level.

A good overall plan for optimum brain health is to devise a brain training regime that incorporates the following:

1. Regular physical exercise, preferably outdoors activities, at least 3 times a week. This boosts your mood and feeds your body with oxygen. It can be something as simple as a brisk walk.

2. Mental challenges such as quizzes, puzzles, and brain training products. There are so many puzzles and products that will stimulate your brain that you will never run out of material to challenge you.

3. Healthy diet. And the good news is, dark chocolate can impact positively on your mood and has antioxidant molecules which stimulate neurological processes that involve learning and memory. Aim for around 35 to 200 grams a day.

4. Supplements such as Ginkgo Biloba are effective for short-term memory improvement and can aid concentration.

5. Good sleeping habits. Attempt to get approximately 8 hours sleep and go to bed at a regular time each night. Doing this helps your body to get into a routine, and you should begin to feel sleepy around the same time every night.

Remember, your brain is your greatest natural resource. Without a healthy brain, you cannot have good health and live your life to the fullest. These are simple steps that anyone can do, but the benefits can be life-changing.

Chapter 2: Applications of Neuroplasticity

The brain is a very powerful organ, and it can store tremendous amounts of information as well as process it. Neuroplasticity has led to several applications that are used by different medical fields. This chapter will discuss the different applications of neuroplasticity.

Treating Brain Damage

Several types of research show that brain plasticity can improve the recovery of the brain from an injury. In fact, many neurologists use brain plasticity in the context of rehabilitating the brain; it is important to take note that the adult brain is not hard-wired with a fixed neural circuit and there are many wirings in the brain that are created in response to injuries. Contrary to what most people believe in, the neural connections do not really die as we age. There is scientific evidence that the cortical, as well as subcortical rewiring in our brain, is the response to training and injury. There is increasing evidence that neurogenesis (the process of creating new brain cells) can also occur in adult mammalian brains.

In one research conducted in 2006, researchers worked with patients who suffered from a stroke which is characterized by the obstruction of the flow of blood to the brain thus affecting the movement of the patient. The research showed that brain injuries caused the reorganization process on the brain thus there is a possibility of using brain plasticity in treating patients suffering from a stroke.

The easiest way to conceptualize neuroplasticity as a treatment for brain damage is to view it as a way to re-learn things. Remember that all throughout your life, the brain always rely on fundamental neurobiological process to acquire behaviors, memories, and experiences. Thus after the brain injury, the brain still has remaining neural circuits that adapt as well as encode new behaviors. Below are the changes that happen after acquired brain injury once a patient undergoes brain plasticity exercises.

•	Increased changes to the synapses such as the synaptogenesis thus the neurons tend to elongate and sprout several projections to create better neural connections.

•	Research also shows increased in neuron growth like specific areas in the hippocampus, dentate gyrus, and sub ventricular zone.

•   Angiogenesis is also stimulated after patients do neuroplasticity exercises. This is the process wherein new blood vessels form from the pre-existing damaged ones. Having enough blood vessels in the brain is crucial because the brain needs Oxygen.

•   The brain also experiences changes in excitability. This refers to the ability of the neurons to generate action potentials which generate electric signals which result in having a strong firing of synapses.

Brain training strengthens the anatomy of the neural connections through sprouting of axons, cortical organization and recruitment of more brain cells.

Improvement of Vision

Brain training has also been reported to improve age-related vision decline. In fact, many doctors now use a visual system training of the brain to allow the brain to compensate for any blurred information captured by the eyes.

Visual plasticity is the ability of the visual system of your brain to adjust its many responses to adapt to the different changes in the visual input. Research showed that practicing with different visual tasks has been known to improve the performance as well as sensitivity to the eyes to a particular vision. When we practice visual exercises, the photoreceptors in the retina are also modified thus causing sensitivity and better performance due to stimulation. This can lead to the prevention of different vision abnormalities such as lazy eye.

As we continue to age, the eyes also begin to perceive blurred images to the brain more than before. Once the brain starts to receive more blurry inputs from your eyes, the details of the images are perceived as having lower contrast compared to reality. For instance, the near vision deterioration, the sensitivity to the initial contrast is lower than usual.

By doing brain plasticity, you are forcing the brain cells of the visual system to interpret visual information at very low contrast thinking that it is the maximum capacity of the brain. Using brain plasticity to treat vision problems promotes cross-talk between the nerve cells and the neuronal circuits of the brain.

Learning Difficulties

People suffering from learning disabilities like dyslexia can benefit from brain plasticity. In a research conducted in patients suffering from age-related cognitive decline (ARCD), patients are required to do six exercises that are designed to reverse the dysfunctions in memory, cognition and motion control. Patients who did the exercise for 8 to 10 weeks showed significant improvement in their performance. Having said this, people who suffer from autism and attention deficit disorder can also take advantage in brain plasticity exercises to improve the state of their learning capabilities.

Chronic Pain

People who suffer from chronic pain due to injury can take advantage of neuroplasticity. During a period of tissue damage, inflammation, as well as noxious stimuli, can elevate the different responses to the central nervous system which, in turn, encourage neuroplasticity response at the cortical level in order to change the somatic organization of the affected painful area thus resulting to central sensitization.

In one research conducted to patients suffering from complex regional pain syndrome showed a reduction of their cortical somatotopic representation and also the volume of the grey matter thus improving the neural connections and improving the desensitization of the affected area. Brain plasticity can be used to treat different chronic pain conditions like phantom limb pain, carpal tunnel syndrome and chronic lower back pain.

The mechanisms that cause chronic pain are poorly understood by scientists. But one thing is clear, and that is people who suffer from chronic pain can benefit from brain plasticity exercises. When individuals undertake tasks like motor training, their performance improves based on the neuroplastic changes in their brain.

Researchers from the Brigham and Women's Hospital in Boston found out that a specific network of brain regions called the Default Mode Network results to changes in neural connections. The study suggests that changes in the brain connectivity reflect a general feature of the chronic pain thus it is important to do exercises that deal with regulating the neural connections that are associated with pain.

Chapter 3: Brain Plasticity Exercises

In order to be healthy, it is not enough to exercise only your body. You also need to exercise your brain. For a long time, many scientists believed that the human brain stops developing during childhood thus we lose neurons every year until we become old. However, the modern research noted that the brain still continues to create neural connections throughout our lives based on our experiences.

Improving the neuroplasticity of the brain through doing brain exercises can help improve the performance and function of your brain despite the presence of factors that can lead to brain damage such as environmental stress, drugs, aging, and growth factors. Just like doing aerobic training for your heart, it is also important to regularly condition your brain by doing daily brain exercises.

Benefits of Regular Brain Exercises

There are many benefits of doing regular brain exercises that translate to better cognitive functioning and performance. Below are the benefits of doing brain exercises to improve the neuroplasticity of the brain.

•	Doing brain exercises can protect your brain from stress. Stress is known to reduce the neuroplasticity of the brain. When the body is stressed, the geometric lengths of the dendrites of the neurons tend to get smaller. Once the neurons shrink, it reduces the number of synapses thus also limiting the number of neural connections. The research found out that once the stress is reduced, the synapses can be replaced or grow its length.

•	Brain exercises can also reduce the bouts of depression. Depression, like stress, can cause changes in the shape of the neurons such that they shorten or shrink.

•	Brain exercises can also induce the production of many brain hormones that can help improve not only the mood but also promote the growth of neural connections thus improving neural plasticity of the brain.

The ability of the human brain to regenerate is stimulated more if brain exercises are performed. These are reasons why doing regular brain exercises are important.

Rules for Brain Plasticity Workouts

So you are ready to start exercising your brain. Before you get started, it is important that you know about the cautions and rules to ensure that you are getting most out of your brain exercises. Remember that neurons that are not stimulated well will not reconnect, so it will make all of your attempts futile. Below are the rules that you need to know to ensure that you are getting enough exercises for your brain.

•	Practice regularly. Neurons that are not stimulated enough usually fail to reconnect. This is especially true if you just suffered from brain injuries. It is crucial to start doing neuroplasticity exercises even before your neurons start to die. If you practice regularly, not only will your neural connections flourish but your neurons will also be regenerated according to many studies.

•	Exercises need to be balanced. It is important to take note that repeating brain exercises for countless of times can lead to the overstimulation of the brain cells in targeted areas. Once this happens, this result to the squeezing out of the information of the new neural connections in other areas which may not be necessarily needed by the brain.

•	Look for improvements in your daily functioning. You may improve your neural connections if you do brain games but if you only get exercises out of these games, then you will not be able to continually stimulate your brain. It is important that you include brain exercises in your daily functioning so that even if you are doing simple tasks or routines, your brain is still continually being stimulated.

•	Be cautious of some exercises in the market. There are many brain games that are marketed as neuroplasticity exercises. Despite being branded as such, it is crucial to take note that most of these exercises are not really effective. Make sure that you follow proven neuroplasticity exercises.

How to Improve Brain Plasticity

Improving the neuroplasticity of your brain does not really involve complicated and expensive brain games. In fact, there are many types of exercises that you can do that fit your life without the need for you to spend money. This section will discuss the different types of brain workouts that you can do to improve your neural connections in your daily life.

•	Intellectual activities: Immersing in activities that are stimulating to the brain can provide the workout that you need for your brain. There are many intellectual activities that you can engage in to fire up your neural connections, and these include doing board games, joining debates and enrolling in online courses.

•	Add variety to your tasks: The thing is that usual activity can still challenge your brain by doing things that are beyond your usual task. For instance, if you always hike on a regular trail, you can find a new trail to explore. What happens in your brain when you add variety to your tasks is that you stretch the intellectual capacity of your brain by adding variety to your usual tasks.

•	Do physical activities: Doing physical activities has a lot of benefits to the health of your brain. One of the reasons why doing physical activities is very important for neuroplasticity is that it encourages the brain to pump brain-stimulating hormones. Research has found out those stroke patients who do physical rehabilitative exercises can stimulate the neurons. When they engage in light exercises such as walking, it can strengthen the neural connections that are associated with the movement.

•	Engage in brainwave entertainment: Brainwave entertainments refer to using invisible waves to stimulate the brain. It has been found out that binaural beats can promote the activity of the left and right brain hemisphere which promote brain thinking. Binaural beats refer to frequencies that are below 1000 and 1500 Hz. These beats influence the function of the human brain through the process called "frequency following response" which activates the different sites of the brain. So where can you listen to binaural beats? There are many ways for you to get brainwave entertainment and these include listening to meditation music, the sound of nature and rustling of the leaves due to wind are some of the sources of brainwave entertainment that you can use to improve your brain connection.

•	Meditate: Meditation can help promote brain health by decreasing the anxiety. Since meditation can also boost the production of hormones in the brain, it can help improve the memory, decision-making and attention span. In studies conducted by researchers, they have found out that people who regularly practice meditation are found to have a greater cognitive function by increasing the formation of the gyri which are the folds found on the surface of the brain.

•	Eat omega-3 rich, fatty acid foods: Eating brain foods such as those that contain a lot of Omega-3 fatty acids can reduce the risk of hemorrhagic stroke. Studies also found out that omega-3 fatty acid rich foods can increase the levels of molecules such as the brain-derived neurotrophic factor (BNDF) to improve the neuroplasticity of the brain. This molecule can regulate the growth, survival and the differentiation of the nerve cells.

•	Eat other brain-enhancing foods: Aside from eating foods rich in omega-3 fatty acid, it is also important to eat green leafy vegetables because they contain vitamins and minerals that prevent the onset of dementia. You also need to add nuts into your diet because they are packed with zinc that is known to improve the cognitive performance. Zinc has been found out to regulate the plasticity of the synapses and also protect the brain against free radicals. Other foods that you need to eat include foods rich in folic acid, vitamin B12, and complex carbohydrates as they improve cognitive abilities of the brain by preventing the occurrence of cerebral infarcts.

•	Drink coffee: Drinking coffee has a lot of advantages to people who want to improve their brain plasticity. They contain natural stimulants that can activate the sympathetic nervous system which is the part of the brain that speeds up its cognitive function. It also contains antioxidants that promote recovery of neurons after stress or injury. Research indicated that drinking 8 ounces of black coffee is enough to improve short-term memory and attention span.

•	Do backpacking: When you travel, try to do backpacking so that you will be able to study the streets of the new city that you are in. Neuroimaging studies show that people who do backpacking display good spatial memory than those who rely on a tour guide. The thing is that backpacking allows you to work your brain and, at the same time, enjoy your trip.

•	Chew gum: Chewing gum improves cognitive function, mood and sustained attention according to the Center for Occupational and Health Psychology at Cardiff University. The thing is that whenever you chew gum, it improves your mental alertness and also decreases stress.

•   Exercise to develop muscles: Pumping weights is not only helpful in making your muscles toned, but it can also improve your cognitive capacity. In a study conducted by researchers from the Psychobiology and Exercise Research Center in Brazil, building muscles can increase the brain-derived neurotrophic factor which controls the growth and survival of brain cells. So whenever you lift weights, make sure that you are not only pumping muscles, but you can also improve your brain function.

•   Try doodling: Doodling is a mindless activity, but many experts believe that doodling is a great way to stimulate the brain. Doodling does not only keep your brain stimulated, but it also helps improve neural connections.

•   Let your mind wander off: Some people discourage their mind wandering off. This is not really bad, and many experts say that making your mind wander off just a few minutes can increase your creativity as well as problem-solving skills. Researchers from the Department of Psychological and Brain Sciences at the University of California found out that prospective mind wandering can improve memory as well as stimulate the autobiographical planning. So if you find yourself wandering off, then let it be. It is a very normal thing to do and healthy for your brain to boot.

•   Eat less: Several studies show that reducing your caloric intake does not only help lose weight but can also lower the risk to the development of neurodegenerative diseases. Researchers from the Massachusetts Institute of Technology noted that experimental laboratory rat has 30% more chances of improving their memory and learning skills. If you have low-calorie intake, it activates the enzyme called Sirtuin 1 which protects the brain from age-related diseases.

•   Laugh often: Laughing does not only help dispel depression and anxiety, but it can also increase the amount of Oxygen in the brain. Studies suggest that people who have sunny dispositions in life have better cognitive performance than those who are melancholic.

•   Play video games: Video games can be addictive, but there are benefits to playing video games. Studies show that people who play video games have better visual selective attention and better reaction time and accuracy in handling real-life tasks. So playing video games is no longer a past time but is a great way to improve your brain plasticity.

•   Play chess: Chess has always been known as a popular mind game. Today, many studies have shown the effects of playing chess among children. Children who played chess exhibited enhanced verbal and math skills.

- Read more books: Reading in itself can help keep the brain working. However, reading does not mean reading only the things that you like. If you want to keep your brain healthy through reading, you should try to read difficult materials to stimulate your brain. In fact, many neuroscientists recommend reading mystery novels because they involve complicated storylines due to the mystery of the plot.

- Spice up your food: Eating spicy food can help preserve memory as well as improve cognitive function. The thing is that spices contain polyphenols that have natural antioxidant properties that protect the nervous system. Examples of spices that you should include cinnamon, cumin, sage, and cilantro are great memory boosters thus make sure that you sprinkle your foods with these ingredients.

- Play any musical instrument: Whether you play guitar or a keyboard, playing musical instruments is not only fun, but it is also a great way to increase your neural connections. Studies conducted on the brains of musicians noted that their gray matter of musicians has profound multiregional differences compared to those who do not play music. This indicates their better adaptation for long-term memory and learning.

- Do yoga: Yoga does not only improve your physical state but also your mental as well as spiritual well-being. Several studies have shown that practicing yoga can help elevate the level of GABA in the brain. GABA is a hormone that fights of depression and other mood disorders.

- Drink plenty of water: Your brain cannot function properly if you are dehydrated. Aside from providing oxygen to the brain, water also helps maintain the fluid balance in the brain. Without proper fluid balance, the brain cannot transmit impulses, produce neurotransmitters and secrete hormones.

- Get enough sleep: Getting enough sleep allows you to have better neurobehavioral functions. Moreover, it is also responsible for improving your cognitive abilities, concentration, mood, and attention. On the other hand, researchers also stress the importance of taking naps to improve focus and memory.

- Solve puzzles: The brain requires stimulation at all times. Solving simple puzzle games like Sudoku or crossword puzzles can increase the oxygen delivery as well as glucose uptake of the brain. It also helps release dopamine which indirectly promotes the production of new brain cells.

- Self-hypnosis: Changing your thought process and learning how to switch your focus through self-hypnosis can help one get sharper mind. It can also help increase your tolerance to pain and can also help improve your focus when doing new things.

- Learn a new language: Learning a new language can do wonders for your brain. Studies show that bilingual speakers have a lower risk of developing dementia compared to adults who only speak one language. What happens is that when we learn a new language, our brains become so stimulated that it fires up signals that can promote fast neural connections.

- Nurture positive relationship: So how does nurturing positive relationship help individuals have better neuroplasticity? Social inadequacies caused by dysfunctional relationship can cause stress and anxiety which result to a lot of mental problems particular cognitive decline. Studies show that elderly people who have good social network have reduced rates of cognitive problems compared to those that have poor relationships with other people.

- Engage in good conversation: Engaging in good conversation can improve your memory and cognitive functioning. Psychology professors from the University of Michigan noted that good conversation with other people nurtures positive relationships which can lead to improved cognition and better mood.

- Organize your things: Organizing your things is not only healthy for your body but also your brain. By tidying your stuff, you will be able to improve your cognitive skills because it refreshes your mind on where you put your things thus improving your memory.

- Write by hand: Many people do not know that there are many benefits of writing by hand. Writing by hand can help individuals develop a kinesthetic sense that will allow their brains to process information effectively. Scientists demonstrated that finger movements due to handwriting could activate the large regions of the brain. This region is involved in language, memory as well as thinking.

- Speak out loud: The act of saying things aloud can have positive effects on the brain. Saying things aloud can help improve our memory so if you are preparing for an exam, do not just mumble your words but say it aloud.

•	Think positive: Thinking positively can make your brain more positive thus improving the capacity of your brain to learn and acquire new skills.

•	Quit smoking: Cigarette smoke robs your brain with Oxygen and fills it with free radicals and carbon monoxide. This decreases the cognitive ability by causing injuries on the inner lining of the blood vessels in the brain. This also increases the likelihood of development of stroke as well as cancer.

•	Avoid alcoholic beverages and drugs: People who drink alcoholic beverages and abuse drugs affect the cognition, judgment as well as control. Alcoholic beverages and drugs can also rob off the brain from Oxygen and produces a lot of free radicals to the body thus preventing the formation of new synapses.

There are many things that you can do to improve your brain plasticity, and it is not only doing brain exercises that can benefit your brain. Living a healthy lifestyle coupled with brain exercises can improve neural connections and fire up brain synapses.

Conclusion

The brain cells do not really die contrary to popular beliefs. Even during adulthood, our brain still creates neural connections thus allowing us to learn new things and also adapt to different information. This is caused by the neuroplasticity of the brain which is the ability of the brain to learn and adapt from different experiences. The thing is that having a sharp mind is not an entitlement of young individuals. So whether you are 50 or 60 years, you can still have a sharp mind as long as you take care of your brain. Doing brain exercises can help improve your brain connections.

Thank you for purchasing this book, I hope you will apply the acquired knowledge productively.

Your Free Gift

I wanted to show my appreciation that you support my work so I've put together a free gift for you.

https://goo.gl/6PMJHu

Just visit the link above to download it now

I know you will love this gift

Thanks